The Rebuild

Zero To Hero

Trauma to High Value Man

Poonam Khan

With love and purpose,

Poonam Khan

Becoming a man isn't about age or strength; it's
about owning your choices, leading with integrity,
and standing tall even when it's hard.

Contents

Introduction

Why We Begin Here

Before you become a high-value man—confident, disciplined, grounded in purpose—you must first meet the boy inside you.

This boy is not weak. He's not a burden. He's the part of you that learned how to survive long before you knew what it meant to thrive. He absorbed the confusion, the absence, the criticism, the abandonment. He learned that strength meant silence, that love meant pleasing, that vulnerability meant weakness.

But here's the truth: no man can build something strong on a broken foundation.

To rebuild, you must confront your past—not to dwell in it, but to reclaim your power from it.

What Is Trauma?

Trauma is not just what happened to you—it's what happened inside you as a result.

It's the emotional, psychological, and physiological response to events that were too overwhelming to fully process at the time.

Trauma can come from big, visible wounds—abuse, violence, abandonment. But it also comes from subtle, invisible wounds— emotional neglect, constant criticism, growing up without feeling seen or safe.

There are three types of trauma every man should know:

Acute Trauma – A single, shocking event (e.g., loss, accident, violence).
Chronic Trauma – Ongoing exposure to harmful environments (e.g., bullying, toxic family dynamics).
Complex Trauma – Deep wounds from attachment issues in childhood, often involving caregivers.

How Trauma Affects You as a Man

Unresolved trauma doesn't stay in the past. It shows up every day—in your relationships, reactions, and sense of self.
You might become hyper-independent, trusting no one.

You might numb yourself with distractions, work, porn, substances, or shallow connections.

You might lash out or shut down emotionally when triggered.
You might constantly seek validation, approval, or dominance— without ever feeling whole.

And worst of all? You might think this is just how life is for men.

But that's a lie. A learned belief. A survival mode.

You were not born broken. You were shaped by pain—but you have the power to reshape yourself.

Trauma Lives in the Body

Science confirms what many of us have felt for years:
trauma doesn't just live in our memories; it lives in our
bodies.

Childhood trauma alters brain development. It disrupts
hormones. It rewires our nervous system to stay on high
alert. And left unchecked, it echoes through our
relationships, our self-worth, our reactions—even our
parenting.

You may not remember every painful moment, but your
body does. That tension in your chest, the way you shut
down emotionally, the impulse to prove yourself, the fear
of being "too much" or "not enough"—these are signs of a
wounded boy trying to feel safe.

Chapter 1
The Broken Foundation

- Healing the Inner Boy

- Trauma and the body

- The father wound & masculine confusion

- False masculinity vs. true strength

- Emotional wounds of childhood

- Reparenting the inner boy

- Why casual relationships keep you empty

Activities & Reflections: Letter to your younger self, Emotional inventory, Visualization, Journal prompts

The Father Wound & Masculine Confusion

The absence of a strong, present, emotionally intelligent father figure leaves a wound that many men carry silently.

Some fathers were physically gone. Others were emotionally unavailable, passive, or even abusive. As boys, we naturally looked to them for identity—but when they failed us, we either rejected masculinity or clung to a distorted version of it.

This is how confusion is born.

You were never meant to figure manhood out alone. But now, you get to rewrite that story.

The Parent Wound & Masculine Confusion

One of the most silent, yet deeply rooted, sources of pain
for many men is the parent wound.

Whether it was a father who was absent, critical, violent, or
simply emotionally unavailable…
Or a mother who was overbearing, neglectful, or treated
you like a partner instead of a child…

…these early experiences shape the emotional blueprint
you carry into adulthood.

As children, we look to our parents not just for food and
shelter—but for identity, security, and emotional
grounding. When those needs aren't met in healthy ways,
we grow up confused, guarded, and disconnected from our
core masculine essence.

We might:

- Overperform, hoping to finally earn approval
- Shut down emotionally, equating vulnerability with danger
- Fear abandonment, but sabotage closeness when we get it
- Reject authority or avoid leadership, fearing we'll hurt others like we were hurt

This is where masculine confusion begins.
Without a healthy example of masculinity, many men internalize one of two lies:

1. Masculinity is domination, ego, aggression, and control
2. Masculinity is toxic and should be avoided altogether

Both extremes rob you of your truth. Real masculinity isn't about dominance or disappearance. It's about presence, protection, and purpose.

To rebuild, we must first face this parent wound—not to blame, but to understand. Not to stay stuck in the past, but to unchain ourselves from it.

What Happens to a Boy Who Doesn't Feel Safe or Seen?

When your parents ignore or mishandle your emotional needs, you don't stop loving them...
You stop trusting yourself.

You may grow up believing:

- "I'm only valuable if I succeed."

- "Love always comes with conditions."

- "If I express pain, I'll be rejected or punished." "If I don't stay strong, I'll fall apart."

You carry those beliefs into adulthood—into relationships, leadership, your sense of masculinity.
You build armor. You suppress softness. You confuse control with strength. You look outside yourself to feel like a man.

9

The Root of Masculine Confusion

Masculinity becomes confusing when you've never seen it modeled in a healthy way.
You're left to piece it together from extremes:

False Masculinity: Aggression, ego, domination, avoidance, emotional repression

False Passivity: Shame, emotional collapse, lack of direction or boundaries

Both are masks—reactions to childhood experiences where you felt unsafe, unworthy, or unseen.
But true masculinity doesn't exist in either extreme. It exists in truth, wholeness, and grounded presence.

You Are Not Broken—You Were Shaped

Everything you struggle with now—the fear of intimacy, the need to perform, the inability to relax or lead with calm—isn't who you are. It's who you became to survive a world where your needs were unmet.
And now that you're aware of it, you have the power to change it.

Healing the parent wound isn't about blame. It's about responsibility.
You didn't cause the damage—but it's your job to repair it, because the man you want to become can't emerge until the boy inside you is finally seen, heard, and healed.

False Masculinity vs. True Strength

Rewriting the Masculine Code You Were Given. As boys, we aren't handed a manual for manhood.

We're handed messages—loud ones, quiet ones, and some so subtle they become invisible.

Messages like:

- "Don't be soft."

- "Real men don't cry."

- "Toughen up."

- "Handle it yourself."

- "Get the girl, get the money, get the status—then you'll matter."

We internalize these rules before we even understand what masculinity is.

We watch how our fathers move.
How they handle anger.
How they show (or don't show) affection.
We absorb what our culture celebrates and mocks.
We learn to perform… instead of being.

And if we don't question those lessons, we spend our adult lives chasing a version of masculinity that keeps us empty, disconnected, and exhausted.

What Is False Masculinity?

False masculinity is a performance.
It's a shell. It's survival mode disguised as strength.

It looks like:

- Aggression instead of boundaries
- Control instead of emotional leadership
- Ego instead of confidence
- Avoidance instead of vulnerability
- Conquest instead of connection
- Numbing instead of feeling

It's the man who talks loudest, but can't sit in silence with himself.
The man who needs validation from women, money, or attention—but has no real self-worth.
The man who's emotionally shut down and calls it "being strong."
The man who fears softness, not knowing it's where true power begins.

False masculinity teaches men to:

- Prioritize image over integrity
- Dominate rather than lead
- Dismiss emotional pain instead of healing it
- Compete with other men instead of building with them
- Treat love like a threat instead of a mirror

So, What Does True Strength Look Like?

True strength isn't loud.
It doesn't need to control the room, impress others, or bury emotion.
True masculinity is rooted, not reactive.
It's a calm, stable, purpose-driven presence—the kind that others feel safe around, not afraid of.

It looks like:

- Owning your emotions without being ruled by them
- Holding yourself accountable, even when it's hard
- Leading with integrity, not performance
- Choosing discipline over instant gratification
- Being protective, not possessive
- Speaking truth with love, not fear

Real masculinity allows for both strength and softness, ambition and emotional depth, independence and connection.
It's not about abandoning your fire—it's about learning how to channel it with wisdom.

Why This Matters

Until you unlearn false masculinity, you'll be stuck in cycles of:

- Surface-level relationships
- Unexpressed frustration
- Leadership that feels like pressure, not purpose
- Success that feels hollow
- Loneliness, even when you're surrounded by people

You don't have to abandon your masculinity to grow—you just have to reclaim it.

Because becoming a high-value man isn't about what the world tells you to be—it's about becoming the most honest, grounded, and powerful version of yourself.

Emotional Wounds of Childhood

The Scars You Can't See Still Shape the Man You Are

Before you ever learned how to build muscle, earn money, or pursue love...
You were a boy with needs—for comfort, safety, approval, attention, and guidance.

What happened to you in those early years didn't just pass. It landed in your nervous system. It became part of your blueprint.

And when those emotional needs were ignored, rejected, or misunderstood, you developed wounds—not always physical, but deeply psychological and emotional.

What Are Emotional Wounds?

An emotional wound is a deep pain created when something essential for your emotional development is missing or violated.

These wounds can come from:

- Being shamed for showing emotion
- Not being protected from chaos or abuse
- Being compared, criticized, or ignored
- Witnessing a parent's emotional absence or addiction
- Carrying adult responsibilities as a child
- Being taught love is something you must earn

And just like physical injuries, if emotional wounds aren't treated, they fester.
They grow. They shape your personality.
They form the invisible walls between you and your purpose, your partner, your peace.

Common Emotional Wounds in Men:

The Wound of Abandonment
Feeling like no one truly stayed. Leads to fear of intimacy, emotional clinginess, or complete detachment.

The Wound of Rejection
Feeling like your real self was "too much" or "not enough." Creates people-pleasing, perfectionism, or a deep fear of failure.

The Wound of Shame
Feeling unworthy of love or success. Leads to self-sabotage, anger, or hiding parts of who you are.

The Wound of Neglect
Being emotionally starved—unseen, unheard. Results in emotional numbness, isolation, and a lack of self-trust.

The Wound of Invalidation
Being told your feelings weren't real or important. Teaches you to dismiss emotion and value logic at all costs—even when it destroys relationships.

How These Wounds Show Up in Adult Life

You may not remember every painful moment—but your body and behaviors do.

That's why today, you may:

- Push people away even though you crave connection
- Seek validation through sex, money, or power
- Feel like no matter what you achieve, it's never enough.
- Struggle to express emotion, or feel overwhelmed when you try
- Attract partners who mirror your childhood dynamics
- React with anger or withdrawal instead of openness

It's not that you're "damaged."

It's that you've been shaped by pain you were never taught how to name.

The Good News: You Can Heal

Awareness is the beginning of healing.
You are not a prisoner of your past—you're the architect of
your future.

But that future depends on your willingness to turn inward,
face what hurt you, and bring compassion to the younger
version of yourself who didn't get what he needed.

You don't need to carry these wounds into your next
relationship, next opportunity, or next chapter.
You can rewrite the story.
But first—you must understand the original script.

Reparenting the Inner Boy
Becoming the Man You Needed as a Child

There's a part of you—often hidden behind your adult responsibilities, ambitions, and identity—that's still holding pain, confusion, and unmet needs.

This part is the inner boy: the emotional self you developed in your early years.

He's still in there. And whether you realize it or not, he's been quietly shaping the way you love, lead, connect, and cope.

Why Reparenting Matters

If your emotional needs were ignored, rejected, or inconsistently met growing up, then no matter how strong or capable you are today, you're likely operating from a fractured foundation.

Reparenting is the process of giving your inner child what he didn't get back then... today.

It's how you break cycles and rebuild your sense of identity, emotional safety, and self-worth—from the inside out.

What Reparenting the Inner Boy Looks Like

1. **Recognizing Him**
    - Notice where your reactions feel out of proportion.
    - Notice what makes you feel small, defensive, or afraid to be seen.

    These are often signs your inner boy is speaking.

2. **Listening to Him Without Judgment**
    - What did he need?
    - What was he afraid of?
    - What beliefs did he form about himself, love, or the world?

3. **Validating His Pain**

    Instead of dismissing the past with "that's over now," say: "That really hurt. I understand why you felt scared, alone, or unworthy. It wasn't your fault."

4.   Offering What Was Missing

Safety:

"You're not alone anymore."

Encouragement:

"You're good enough as you are."

Nurturing:

"I'm here for you, no matter what."

5.   Creating New Patterns as the Adult You

- Set boundaries he didn't know how to set.
- Make healthy decisions he never had the power to make.
- Speak kindly to yourself, as you would to him.
- Stop abandoning yourself to please others.

You Become the Father He Never Had

Reparenting isn't about blaming your parents forever.
It's about acknowledging what was missing or harmful, and
choosing to stop the damage from continuing through you.

You become the safe place you never had.
You give yourself the voice, the protection, the discipline,
the compassion that your younger self needed.

And when you do this, you stop reacting to life through
pain...
You start responding to it from purpose.
You build emotional maturity.
You reclaim inner peace.
You gain control—not over people or circumstances,
But over yourself.

This is not a weakness.
This is real manhood.

Why Casual Relationships Keep You Empty

You Can't Numb Loneliness With Attention

In today's world, casual relationships are glorified—hookups, flings, "situationships," and temporary connections that feel exciting in the moment but rarely lead to fulfillment.

Many men confuse this with freedom.
But what they often experience is repetition, disconnection, and emptiness.

The Illusion of Power

At first, casual relationships can feel like success:
- You're wanted
- You feel in control
- There's no obligation
- You avoid vulnerability

But underneath that illusion is often a deeper truth:

- You're afraid of being truly seen

- You don't trust yourself to choose well

- You don't know how to lead in emotional intimacy

- You fear rejection or commitment

- You're repeating the very abandonment you once experienced—this time, by doing it to yourself

You end up chasing affection without depth. Validation without vision.

When emotional connection is missing, sex becomes a substitute for:

- Love

- Comfort

- Belonging

- Meaning

- Security

But physical closeness can never fill emotional emptiness.
So you stay hungry.
You stay restless.
You keep searching.

And every time a casual relationship ends, it reinforces the story that "real love doesn't last," or worse—that you're not made for it.

It becomes a loop:

Desire → Excitement → Surface Connection → Withdrawal→ Emptiness → Repeat

This isn't because you're broken.
It's because you're trying to meet deep emotional needs with shallow substitutes.

The Real Cost of Casual

- You lose time you can't get back
- You become emotionally numb
- You miss the opportunity to experience real partnership
- You confuse attention with love
- You train yourself to stay in survival, not build in purpose

And here's the truth:

The more you entertain what isn't aligned, the longer you delay what's meant for you.

What Real Connection Requires

If you want more than temporary validation, you need to:
- Heal the wounds that taught you love wasn't safe

- Learn to regulate your emotions and desires

- Recognize your worth without needing constant approval

- Lead with integrity, not impulse

- Build relationships rooted in shared values and emotional safe

The path to high-value masculinity isn't paved with options—
It's built on intentionality.

And when you rise above the noise of distraction, you'll be shocked at the depth of connection, power, and peace that become available to you.

What Real Connection Requires

- Healing your attachment wounds—not denying them

- Emotional maturity—not emotional avoidance

- Boundaries—not barriers

- Purpose—not impulse

- The courage to risk being known—not just being desired

The Truth You Need to Hear
The right person will not cost you your peace.
The right relationship will not diminish your freedom—it will deepen your power.

But first, you must become the man who's no longer afraid to be seen, supported, and loved.

Because true masculinity isn't built through pleasure…
It's built through purpose, integrity, and the kind of love that calls you higher.

You Can't Numb Loneliness with Attention

In today's world, casual relationships are glorified—
hookups, flings, "situationships," and temporary
connections that feel exciting in the moment but rarely lead
to fulfillment.
Many men confuse this with freedom.
But what they often experience is repetition, disconnection,
and emptiness.

The Illusion of Power

- At first, casual relationships can feel like success:

- You're wanted

- You feel in control

- There's no emotional obligation

- You avoid vulnerability and risk

In today's world, casual relationships are glorified—

Hookups, flings, "situationships," and temporary connections that
But under that surface is often a deeper truth:

- You're afraid of being truly seen

- You don't trust yourself to choose a healthy partner

- You fear giving someone power to hurt you

- You don't feel equipped to lead in emotional intimacy
- You're repeating the very abandonment you once experienced—this time, by abandoning yourself

You end up chasing physical closeness while avoiding emotional depth.
And each time something ends, it confirms the false story:

"See? Nothing lasts."
"See? I'm not built for love."

The Real Reason You Fear Commitment

For many men, the avoidance of deep, long-term relationships isn't about disinterest—
it's about fear.

You may have been:
Betrayed by someone you trusted
Abandoned after opening your heart
Mocked for your emotions
Manipulated or controlled by someone close
Now intimacy feels dangerous, Vulnerability feels like weakness.
And commitment feels like a risk you're not sure you can survive again.

Let down repeatedly—even by family—
you began to believe:

"If I don't go deep, I can't get hurt."
"If I keep it casual, I stay in control."
"Real love is a trap, not a gift."

But that's not protection.
That's prison.

Your past pain doesn't mean you're incapable of love.
It just means your capacity for love hasn't been met with
the right healing and the right person yet.

Being hurt in the past is not proof that love is unsafe
It's a sign that something inside you was crying out for
growth.

◆ Activities & Reflections

1.   Letter to Your Younger Self

Write a heartfelt letter to the child you once were.
Acknowledge the pain he endured.
Offer him the love, protection, and encouragement he
needed to hear.
End the letter by promising to protect him moving forward.

2.   Emotional Inventory

List the major emotional wounds you remember (e.g., neglect, rejection, shame).
For each, answer:

- What triggered it?

- How did I feel?

- How did I react?

- What belief did I form about myself?

3.   Visualization Exercise

Close your eyes. Visualize your younger self in a safe,
loving space.
Imagine an adult-you entering that space, embracing him,
and saying:

"You're safe now."
"You're not alone."
"You were always enough."

Breathe deeply and anchor that safety into your body.

4. Journal Prompts

- What did I need as a child that I didn't receive?
- What patterns in my life stem from those unmet needs?
- Who do I become when I feel unworthy or unsafe?
- What does the man I'm becoming say to the boy I was?

Chapter 2

Reclaiming Masculinity – The Strength in Structure
Becoming the Man Who Builds, Leads, and Protects

Masculinity is not lost, it's buried.
Buried beneath trauma, culture, confusion, and
performance.
Buried beneath shame, fear of being "too much," or fear of
becoming like the men who hurt us.

Most men never had a healthy model of masculinity. They
were taught to suppress, to chase, to conquer, to avoid
emotion and call it "strength."
Or they saw so much chaos and abuse from male figures
that they rejected masculinity altogether.

Becoming the Man Who Builds, Leads, and Protects

Masculinity is not lost—it's buried.
Buried beneath trauma, culture, confusion, and
performance.
Buried beneath shame, fear of being "too much," or fear of
becoming like the men who hurt them.

And now? Many men walk around feeling directionless,
disconnected, or like they're living someone else's life.
They feel either too soft or too cold. Too passive or too
dominant. Too emotional or not emotional enough.

Because no one ever told them this:

>   Masculinity is not about power over others. It's
about power over self.

Real masculinity is calm. It's disciplined. It's grounded.
It doesn't need to control—it creates structure.
It doesn't need to impress—it creates presence.
It doesn't need to perform—it creates protection.

Why You Must Reclaim Your Masculinity

If you don't define masculinity for yourself, the world will
do it for you—and it will get it wrong.

You'll either:

Become the man who dominates out of insecurity
Or
the man who disappears out of fear
But your future family doesn't need either.
Your mission doesn't need either.
You don't need either.

You need to become the man who builds.
Who leads with love, not ego.
Who protects what's sacred.
Who creates vision, clarity, and calm even when the world is on fire.

This chapter is your return to that man.
Not through ego. Not through chasing external status.
But through internal order.

Because until you are structured within, everything around you will stay chaotic.

This is where the rebuild becomes real.

What True Masculinity Looks Like
Change, Adaptation & The Power of Structure

The man you were taught to be and the man you're meant to become are not the same.

Becoming the man you were created to be requires a conscious shift—a reprogramming of old beliefs, habits, and behaviors.

It requires unlearning the survival traits that once protected you and replacing them with principles that elevate you.

This isn't just about self-improvement.
This is about reclaiming your design—and operating from strength instead of struggle.

Change Without Structure Doesn't Last

You can read the books. Listen to the podcasts. Set the goals.
But if your life has no structure—no guiding principles—your change won't stick.

That's why so many men start strong and then fall off. It's not because they're lazy. It's because their growth isn't grounded.

Masculinity needs structure the way a house needs a frame. Without it, everything collapses under pressure.

You can't lead your emotions, your relationships, or your mission without order.
And order begins with discipline and principle.

Discipline: The Gatekeeper of Masculine Power

Let's get this clear:
>   Discipline is not punishment.
>   Discipline is self-respect in motion.

When you say you'll do something and you follow through, you build trust with yourself.
And every time you break your word, every time you procrastinate, lie to yourself, or fold under pressure—you weaken your masculine core.

Discipline is how you build internal power. It's how you move from reaction to response.
From distraction to direction.
From chaos to clarity.

If you want to become unshakable, start by mastering your mornings, your mind, your mouth, and your emotions.

The Four Pillars of Masculinity

True masculinity isn't vague.
It's not about outdated stereotypes or shallow performance.
It's built on pillars—stable, time-tested foundations that create internal strength and external leadership.

Here are the four pillars you must integrate:

1.   Structure
You create order in your life.
You are intentional with your time, actions, and boundaries.
You bring clarity to confusion.

Without structure, you drift.
With structure, you dominate your day.

2.   Presence

You are grounded, focused, and emotionally available.
You don't disappear during conflict or seek escape when things get hard.
Your presence is a gift—people feel safe around a man who is present.

3.   Direction

You know where you're going.
You lead with a vision.
You make decisions from alignment, not anxiety.

Men without direction chase distraction
Men with direction build a legacy.

4.   Protection

You protect what matters—your peace, your purpose, your
relationships, and your energy.
You are a safe place, not just a strong one.
You don't control. You cover.
You don't dominate. You defend.

Why These Pillars Matter

Without these pillars, a man becomes reactive, restless, and
unstable.
He's blown around by circumstances. He's ruled by
emotion or ego.
He either overcompensates—or completely checks
out.

But with these pillars, a man becomes stable, trustworthy,
and powerful.
He doesn't just survive—he leads. He builds. He anchors
others.

And that kind of man?

He doesn't need to prove his masculinity.
He embodies it.

Building Self-Discipline & Emotional Control
How a Man Builds Inner Authority
Every man wants to feel powerful.
But real power isn't built in the gym, in your bank account,
or through status.
It's built in the silent moments—when no one is watching,
and the only one you must answer to… is yourself.

Self-Discipline Is Self-Trust

You cannot lead others—your partner, your business, your family—if you cannot lead yourself.
And self-leadership begins with discipline.

Most people think discipline is about restriction.
But real discipline is freedom—because when you master your habits, you stop being a slave to your impulses.

>   Discipline says:
"I do what's necessary, even when it's uncomfortable."
"I honor my word, even when no one sees it."
"I'm committed to who I want to become, not what I feel in the moment."

Every time you follow through on your word, you tell your inner boy,
"I've got you. You can trust me now."
That's how self-respect is built—one decision at a time.

Why Most Men Lack Discipline

It's not because they're lazy.
It's because they've never been taught to feel pain without escaping it.

Without emotional tools, boys grow into men who:

- Avoid discomfort with distractions (porn, scrolling, overeating, substances)
- Start things they never finish
- Sabotage progress when it gets boring or hard
- Let their mood decide their behavior
- Crave motivation instead of building consistency

But here's the truth:

Motivation is emotional. Discipline is structural.
Motivation gets you going. Discipline keeps you growing.

Emotional Control: Feeling Without Losing Yourself
True masculinity is not emotionally numb. It's emotionally
mature.

- Emotional control is not suppression—it's
  leadership.

It means:
- You feel anger, but don't explode.

- You feel sadness, but don't collapse.

- You feel fear, but still move forward.

- You feel desire, but don't abandon your values.

The Cost of Emotional Immaturity

- When a man doesn't master his emotions, he:

- Destroys relationships with reactivity or shutdown

- Makes poor decisions based on impulse

- Feels constant shame and regret

- Blames others for his triggers

- Lives in cycles of guilt and avoidance

Emotional immaturity leaves a man feeling powerless in his own life.
But when you build the muscle of emotional self-regulation, you earn something more valuable than control over others: control over yourself.

Daily Practices to Build Discipline & Emotional Strength

- Wake up on your first alarm. Start the day with integrity.
- Train your body. Physical mastery fuels mental resilience.
- Limit your vices. Trade dopamine for discipline.
- Journal your thoughts. Learn to process, not suppress.
- Meditate or breathe daily. Anchor your nervous system.
- Delay gratification. Strengthen your patience and control.
- Finish what you start. Prove to yourself that you are dependable.

Discipline and emotional control don't make you less of a man—

they make you a man others can depend on.
And more importantly?
They make you a man you can depend on.

Being Powerful and Grounded
How True Strength Is Built Through Stillness, Not Noise

Power. It's something every man wants to feel. But what most don't realize is this:

Power doesn't come from being loud. It comes from being rooted.

In a world full of noise, performance, and comparison, true masculine power is quiet.
It's steady. It's composed. It's grounded.

It's the kind of presence that doesn't have to announce itself... because it's felt.

What It Means to Be Grounded

To be grounded means:

You are not easily shaken by other people's moods or

opinions

You respond instead of react

You don't chase validation—you live from your core

You walk into rooms with calm certainty, not ego

You hold your frame, even when tested

Being grounded is what separates boys from men.

It's the trait that allows you to lead in love, remain stable in crisis, and make decisions from truth, not triggers.

Why Many Men Confuse Noise With Strength

Growing up, most of us were shown false images of power:
- The loudest guy wins the room
- Control equals confidence
- Dominance equals leadership
- Stoicism means silence

So what do men do?
They overcompensate. They puff up. They perform. They disconnect. They intimidate.

But real strength has nothing to prove.

Real strength is the man who can sit in silence and still feel solid.
Real strength is the man who can hear criticism without collapsing
 Real strength is the man who doesn't need the last word— because he knows who he is.

Grounded Power in Practice

To be powerful and grounded, you must:

Know your values – what you stand for, what you protect, what you walk away from

Live with rhythm – routines that stabilize your mind, body, and emotions

Stay present in discomfort – without needing to numb, attack, or run

Stand firm in conflict – with calm, clear communication

Connect to purpose – because men without purpose chase pleasure

When a man is grounded, he becomes a force.
Not because of his dominance—but because of his
discipline, direction, and depth.

The Masculine Trinity: Power + Peace + Presence

The highest version of masculinity is not just powerful. He is also peaceful and present.

Power gives him strength.
Peace gives him self-trust.
Presence gives him impact.

And when those three qualities combine—you become a man that others respect, follow, and feel safe around... not because you demand it, but because you embody it.

This is what it means to be both strong and safe. Firm, but not forceful.
Grounded, but not passive.
Open-hearted, but never out of control.

The Role of Men in Relationships and Society

How to Lead with Strength, Purpose, and Integrity

In every home, every relationship, every community—
masculinity matters.
Not because men are better.
Not because they deserve power.
But because when masculinity is healthy, it brings
something irreplaceable to the world:

Safety. Direction. Stability. Protection. Legacy.

Yet many men today feel confused, silenced, or ashamed to step into this role.
Why?

Because masculinity has either been:
- Distorted into domination and control

Or
- Dismissed as toxic and unnecessary

The result?

A generation of men who are either:
- Too passive or too aggressive...
- Too disconnected or too dominating...
- Too afraid to lead or too reckless to follow through.

But masculinity, at its highest form, is not a threat. It's a blessing.

What the World Needs From You

The world doesn't need another man chasing status,
performing ego, or avoiding responsibility.
The world needs a man who:

- Shows up consistently

- Leads with vision

- Stands firm in values

- Protects what matters

- Serves without needing applause

- Loves with discipline and truth

- Builds legacy instead of chasing validation

That King isn't born.
He's forged—through fire, humility, healing, and
leadership.

Your Role in Relationships

In a healthy relationship, the man isn't meant to
dominate—he's meant to lead with love.
This doesn't mean control.
It means carrying the weight of responsibility.

It means:
- Taking initiative without expecting praise

- Holding space for emotion while staying grounded

- Setting the tone for vision, direction, and trust

- Offering protection—not just physically, but
  emotionally

- Being decisive, present, and emotionally available

- Building safety through consistency—not perfection

You don't need to be perfect.
You need to be solid.
You need to be accountable.
You need to be growing.

Because the woman, the children, the people in your care—
will rise or fall with your consistency, not your charm..

Your Role in Society

Every man has influence—whether he accepts it or not.

You influence:
- The way boys learn to express emotion

- The way women experience safety

- The way leadership is modeled

- The way responsibility is carried

You Are Not "Just a Man."

You are a builder of homes, families, movements, and legacy.

When you walk in your masculine leadership, others feel it. They may not always agree with you—
but they will respect you… because you're clear, grounded, and aligned.

Stepping Into That Role
To truly embrace your role as a leader:

- Define your values. Let them shape every decision.

- Lead yourself first—your habits, emotions, and relationships.

Protect your peace—so you can protect others from chaos.
Speak truth with love—even when it's uncomfortable.
Serve your mission—not your ego.
Show up when it's hard—not just when it's convenient.

You weren't made to shrink.
You were made to build, cover, and rise.

Your strength is not a threat.
When aligned with integrity—it's a gift.

The Role of Men in Relationships and Society
How to Lead with Strength, Purpose, and Integrity

In every home, every relationship, every community—
masculinity matters.

Not because men are better.
Not because they deserve power.
But because when masculinity is healthy,
It brings something irreplaceable to the world:

Safety. Direction. Stability. Protection. Legacy.

Yet many men today feel confused, silenced, or ashamed to
step into this role.

Why?

Because masculinity has either been:

- Distorted into domination and control

Or

- Dismissed as toxic and unnecessary

The result?

A generation of men who are either

- Too passive or too aggressive…
- Too disconnected or too dominating…
- Too afraid to lead or too reckless to follow through.

But masculinity, at its highest form, is not a threat. It's a blessing.

What the World Needs From You

The world doesn't need another man chasing status,
performing ego, or avoiding responsibility.
The world needs a man who:

- Shows up consistently

- Leads with vision Stands firm in values

- Protects what matters

- Serves without needing applause

- Loves with discipline and truth

- Builds legacy instead of chasing validation

That man isn't born.
He's forged—through fire, humility, healing, and
leadership.

That man isn't born
He's forged—through fire, humility, healing, and
leadership.

Your Role in Relationships

In a healthy relationship, the man isn't meant to
dominate—
he's meant to lead with love.
This doesn't mean control.
It means carrying the weight of responsibility.
It means:

- Taking initiative without expecting praise

- Holding space for emotion while staying grounded

- Setting the tone for vision, direction, and trust

- Offering protection—not just physically, but
  emotionally

Being decisive, present, and emotionally available Building safety through consistency—not perfection
You don't need to be perfect.
You need to be solid.
You need to be accountable.
You need to be growing.

Because the woman, the children, the people in your care—will rise or fall with your consistency, not your charm.

Your Role in Society
Every man has influence—whether he accepts it or not.
You influence:

- The way boys learn to express emotion

- The way women experience safety

- The way leadership is modeled

- The way responsibility is carried

- The way conflict is handled

- The way strength is defined

You are not **"just a man."**
You are not **"just a man."**

You are a builder of homes, families, movements, and legacy.

When you walk in your masculine leadership, others feel it. They may not always agree with you—but they will respect you...
because you're clear, grounded, and aligned.

Stepping Into That Role

To truly embrace your role as a leader:

- Define your values. Let them shape every decision.

- Lead yourself first—your habits, emotions, and relationships.

- Protect your peace—so you can protect others from chaos.

- Speak truth with love—even when it's uncomfortable.

- Serve your mission—not your ego.

- Show up when it's hard—not just when it's convenient.

You weren't made to shrink.
You were made to build, cover, and rise.

Your strength is not a threat.
When aligned with integrity—it's a gift.

Conclusion: Becoming the Man the World Needs— Starting With You

Masculinity is not toxic.
Wounded masculinity is.
Absent masculinity is.
Performative masculinity is.

But healed, grounded, disciplined masculinity?
That is sacred.
And the world is starving for it.

We are in a time when many men have forgotten who they are.
Some are performing to be liked.
Others are hiding to avoid responsibility.
Many are carrying wounds they never asked for,
repeating cycles they never meant to repeat.

But the pain stops with you.

Conclusion: Becoming the Man the World Needs—
Starting With You

Masculinity—
Not by rejecting masculinity—but by rebuilding it.

- By becoming the man:

- Who keeps his word

- Who protects, not controls

- Who leads with vision and heart

- Who disciplines himself so others don't have to

- Who walks into rooms and brings calm—not chaos

- Who builds something bigger than himself

This chapter was not just about reclaiming some abstract ideal—
it's about reclaiming yourself.

Because once a man has structure, presence, direction, and discipline,
He becomes unshakable.

He stops chasing respect… because he already walks in it.
He stops fearing rejection… because he no longer abandons himself.
He stops proving he's a man… because he embodies it.

This is the kind of man who commands a room without a word.
The kind of man a good woman can trust.
The kind of man a child feels safe around.
The kind of man who changes the world—not through force, but through example.

The kind of man you're becoming.

Chapter 2
Activities & Reflections: Reclaiming Masculinity – The Strength in Structure

1. The Masculine Blueprint Journal
Prompt:
- What were you taught about masculinity growing up?
- Who were the male role models in your life? What did you learn from them—both good and bad?
- What behaviors did you adopt that you now realize were based on survival, ego, or confusion?

Write a full page reflecting on the "code" of masculinity you were given vs. the man you want to become.

2. The 4 Pillars Audit

Rate yourself from 1 to 10 on the following pillars of masculinity
(1 = weak, 10 = strong):

- Structure: How intentional and disciplined is your day-to-day life?

- Presence: How often are you fully in the moment— with people, emotions, tasks?

- Direction: Do you have a clear vision for your future and act in alignment with it?

- Protection: How well do you protect your peace, time, energy, and values?

- Reflection: Which area is your weakest? What steps can you take this week to improve it?

3. The Self-Discipline Tracker (7-Day Challenge)

Create a simple daily habit tracker with the following actions:

- Wake up on first alarm
- 30 minutes of physical activity
- 10 minutes of meditation or breathwork
- 1 act of delayed gratification (saying no to a distraction)
- Journaling or reflection

Task:
Complete this for 7 consecutive days.
Track your wins.
At the end of the week, Write down how your mindset, emotions, or energy shifted through the process.

◆ **4. The Environment Cleanse**

List out the following

3 habits
3 people
3 digital distractions

...that are keeping you in a state of confusion, chaos, or ego-driven behavior.

Next Step:
Choose 1 from each category to reduce or eliminate this week.

Reflection Prompt:
Write about how this change supports the man you're becoming
What do you notice in your focus, energy, or sense or peace?

Chapter 3
Emotional Power–Learning to Connect, Not Control

Why Your Emotions Are Not the Enemy

If Chapter 2 gave you the foundation to stand firm, then Chapter 3 will give you the ability to stand open
—without collapsing.

Most men were never taught what to do with their emotions. They were taught to control them.
Or ignore them.
Or drown in them.

So it's no surprise that emotional overwhelm, numbness, and rage
are epidemic among men.

And when you're emotionally untrained, the people around you feel it—
especially in your relationships, your leadership, and your inner peace.
But here's the truth:

But here's the truth:

Emotional intelligence is not weakness. It is power
And when a man learns to own his emotions—without
being ruled by them—
he becomes unstoppable.

The Old Model: Suppress, Perform, Explode

From a young age, many boys are told:

"Stop crying."

"Get over it."

"Don't be soft."

"Man up."

"No one cares how you feel."

So what do we do?
We suppress emotion to appear strong.
We perform strength through silence, aggression, or
withdrawal.And eventually, we explode—in anger,
resentment, or breakdown.

This model keeps men emotionally stunted—
capable of building businesses or bodies,
but unable to connect with their partners, children, or even
themselves.

You can't lead others if you can't even lead your own
nervous system.

The New Model: Feel, Own, Lead

Emotional power doesn't mean crying all the time.
It means becoming fluent in your internal world so that
emotions become messengers—not masters.

To reclaim your emotional power, you must learn to:

- Feel fully – without judging, suppressing, or
  bypassing
- Own your reactions – and take responsibility for
  how you respond

- Lead through emotional presence – especially during conflict or chaos

- Communicate what's real – instead of manipulating or shutting down

- Create emotional safety – for yourself and others

Why Emotional Intelligence Is Strength, Not Weakness
The Hidden Superpower of Masculine Leadership

For generations, men were taught that emotions were something to hide.
They were told strength meant being stoic, silent, and self-contained.

But that version of strength was never about power—it was about survival.

It was about protecting yourself in a world that told you emotions make you soft, feminine, or unfit to lead.

And so, you learned to suppress what made you human.
You traded connection for control.
Vulnerability for performance.
Truth for silence.

But here's the reality:

It takes more strength to feel than to flee. More strength to be honest than to hide.
More strength to stand in your emotion without shame than to bury it in ego.

This is what emotional intelligence actually is.
And for a man—it's not just powerful…
it's essential.

What Is Emotional Intelligence?
Emotional intelligence (EQ) is your ability to:

1.   Recognize what you're feeling

2.   Understand where it's coming from

3.   Regulate your response

4.   Communicate it clearly

5.   Respond to others with awareness and empathy

It's not about being emotionally reactive.
It's about being emotionally responsible.

And when a man develops Emotional Intelligence,
he becomes:

More confident

More connected

More calm under pressure

More effective in conflict

More powerful in communication

More trustworthy in leadership

Because people—especially your partner or your
children—don't feel safe around silence or rage.
They feel safe around a man who can hold his center
without avoiding the truth.

Why Emotional Intelligence Is Strength, Not Weakness
The Hidden Superpower of Masculine Leadership

For generations, men were taught that emotions were
something to hide.
They were told strength meant being stoic, silent, and self-contained.

But that version of strength was never about power—it was
about survival.

It was about protecting yourself in a world that told you
emotions make you soft, feminine, or unfit to lead.

And so, you learned to suppress what made you human.
You traded connection for control.
Vulnerability for performance.
Truth for silence.

But here's the reality:

It takes more strength to feel than to flee. More strength to be honest than to hide.
More strength to stand in your emotion without shame than to bury it in ego.

This is what emotional intelligence actually is.
And for a man—it's not just powerful...
it's essential.

What Is Emotional Intelligence?
Emotional intelligence (EQ) is your ability to:

1.   Recognize what you're feeling

2.   Understand where it's coming from

3.   Regulate your response

4.   Communicate it clearly

5.   Respond to others with awareness and empathy

It's not about being emotionally reactive.
It's about being emotionally responsible.

Emotional Intelligence in Real Life

Here's how EQ looks in your daily life:

You recognize you're feeling anxious before a big decision. Instead of hiding it, you breathe, reflect, and respond with clarity.

Your partner brings up something emotional. You don't shut down. You stay present and curious.

You get angry—but instead of lashing out, you name it. You ground yourself. You speak from truth, not reaction.

You notice a friend struggling.
Instead of giving advice or changing the subject, you hold space.
You listen. You validate.

These are not small things.
These are leadership traits.
These are relationship skills.
These are warrior-level strengths.

Emotional Intelligence Builds Masculine Confidence
Would you like help expanding on how EQ translates into confidence and stability in leadership, relationships, or purpose?

A man who is emotionally aware:

- Doesn't fear being misunderstood—he knows how to communicate.

- Doesn't fear confrontation—he knows how to stay grounded.

- Doesn't need to prove himself—he knows who he is.

- Doesn't collapse under pressure—he regulates, reflects, and leads.

He becomes a rock for his family.
A mirror for his woman.
A force in his community.
And a king in his own life.

Identifying Emotional Triggers & Healing Reactive Patterns
Turning Your Triggers Into Tools for Growth

Every man has triggers.

Moments when he feels disrespected, abandoned, attacked, dismissed, or unsafe—
and suddenly, he's no longer the calm, grounded version of himself.

Maybe it's when someone questions your ability.
Maybe it's when your partner pulls away emotionally.
Maybe it's when someone talks over you, ignores you, or challenges your authority.

Whatever it is, that moment isn't just about now.
It's about then.

Because triggers aren't created by the present.
They're activated by the present—but created by the past.

Maybe it's when someone questions your ability.
Maybe it's when your partner pulls away

>   Triggers are emotional echoes—reminders of a
wound that was never fully healed.

And until you identify and heal those wounds,
you'll keep repeating the same reactions—even when you
know better.

What Is a Trigger?

A trigger is an emotional reaction that's disproportionate to
the current moment.
It feels intense, sudden, and hard to control.
It pulls you out of your logical mind and into emotional
survival: fight, flight, freeze, or fawn.

- Lead through emotional presence— especially during conflict or chaos.

- Communicate what's real—instead of manipulating or shutting down.

- Create emotional safety—for yourself and others.

Why Emotional Intelligence Is Strength, Not Weakness
The Hidden Superpower of Masculine Leadership

For generations, men were taught that emotions were something to hide.
They were told strength meant being stoic, silent, and self contained.

But that version of strength was never about power —
It was about survival.

Here's what it might look like:

- You shut down emotionally during conflict

- You get irrationally angry when you feel ignored

- You become anxious or clingy when someone takes space

- You lash out when your authority is questioned

- You feel unworthy when you make a mistake

These aren't character flaws.
They're defense systems—built by the inner boy who learned, somewhere along the way,
that he wasn't safe.

How Triggers Form

- Most emotional triggers are rooted in:

- Childhood emotional neglect

- Shame-based parenting

- Unpredictable or emotionally unstable households

- Early relationships where trust was broken

- Repeated rejection, bullying, or failure

Your body and brain learned:

"Next time something like this happens, I'll protect myself before I get hurt."

So now, even as a grown man, you react—
not to the person in front of you,
but to the pain behind you.

Healing Begins With Awareness

You can't heal what you don't name.
So the first step is to become curious, not critical.

Ask yourself:

- "What situations make me feel emotionally unsafe?"
- "What's the first emotion I feel when I get triggered?"
- "What does this remind me of from earlier in life?"
- "What belief does this trigger activate in me?" ("I'm not enough," "I'm going to be left," "I have to be perfect," etc.)
- "How do I normally react—and what is it trying to protect me from?"

This isn't about blaming others.
It's about understanding the origin of the pattern
so you can stop passing it forward.

The Healing Process

1.   Recognize the Pattern
Before you can change anything, you have to see it clearly. Write down your common triggers, emotional reactions, and where you think they come from.

2.   Sit With the Emotion
Instead of pushing it away or escaping into distraction— breathe into it. Let it rise. Give it space. Feel it in your body. Most emotions pass in under 90 seconds if you let them move.

3.   Speak to Your Inner Boy
This is where reparenting comes in. When you feel the trigger rise, imagine speaking to the boy inside who first felt this pain.

Tell him:

"You're safe now. You're not alone. I see you. I've got you."

4.   Reframe the Belief

What lie is the trigger telling you?
Replace it with truth:

"I am not powerless."
"I am not that helpless child anymore."
"I can respond with wisdom, not fear."

5.   Practice New Responses

The next time you feel triggered:

- Pause

- Breathe

- Acknowledge the emotion

- Respond with intention

You may not get it perfect at first.
That's okay.

Healing is messy—but progress is power.

What Changes When You Heal

When you do this work consistently, your entire experience of life shifts:

- You stop overreacting to little things
- You become more emotionally available in your relationships
- You handle criticism without collapsing
- You no longer fear conflict—you welcome it with clarity You feel safer in your body, your decisions, and your
- leadership

This is what makes a man emotionally powerful.

Not the absence of emotion—but the ability to hold it, lead it, and use it for growth.

You stop being ruled by your past.
You stop hurting the people you love.
And you finally stop abandoning yourself.

Communicating Feelings Without Shame or Manipulation
Speaking Truth Without Losing Power

Most men were never taught how to talk about their feelings—only how to avoid them, hide them, or explode them.

So when emotion comes up, it often feels like a threat:

- A threat to their authority.

- A threat to their image.

But here's the truth:

> Communicating feelings doesn't make you less of a
> man. It makes you a man others can finally
> understand, trust, and connect with.

Why Most Men Struggle to Communicate Emotion
Men often default to two extremes:

1. **Silence** – shutting down to avoid conflict or
   discomfort

2. **Explosion** – lashing out after bottling up too long

In both cases, the root issue is the same:
You don't feel safe expressing the truth without losing
control or being rejected.

So you either hide your needs... or try to force them to be
met.

But neither is communication.
One is avoidance.
The other is manipulation.

True communication happens between those who feel safe enough to be real—and skilled enough to stay responsible.

What Healthy Emotional Communication Looks Like
1. Start With Ownership
Use "I" statements—not accusations.

Instead of: "You make me feel ignored."
Say: "I feel hurt when I don't hear from you. I value connection, and silence makes me anxious."

You're not blaming. You're revealing.

2. Name the Emotion Without Shame
You're allowed to say:

- "I feel overwhelmed."

- "I feel disconnected."

- "I feel disappointed."

- "I feel insecure right now."

These are signs of self-awareness—not weakness.

3. Speak to Be Understood—Not to Win
This isn't a courtroom. It's a connection. The goal is to be heard, not to dominate.
Drop the ego. Keep the honesty.

Don't weaponize your pain to gain control.
Don't guilt-trip or play the victim.
Don't overshare just to get a reaction.

Healthy communication is about expression, not emotional leverage.

5. Stay Regulated
Emotional honesty doesn't mean emotional chaos. If you feel dysregulated, pause. Breathe. Re-center.
Then speak from your calm, grounded self—not your triggered self.

Masculine Communication in Action

Let's say you feel neglected in your relationship.

Here's the unhealthy response:

"You never care. You always ignore me. I'm done."

Here's the grounded, emotionally intelligent version:

"Lately I've been feeling distant. I've been craving more connection and presence between us. Can we talk about how we can both show up better?"

Same situation.
Completely different energy.
One creates division.
The other invites reconnection.

Why It Matters

Every time you communicate clearly, calmly, and honestly, you:

- Build trust with your partner
- Create emotional safety
- Model healthy leadership
- Stop the cycles of miscommunication that break most relationships
- Become a man who can be understood—not just obeyed or avoided

And that kind of man?
He's magnetic. Powerful. Respected. Relatable.
Because he leads with truth—not fear.
And he makes connection safe and strong—instead of complicated and chaotic.

Replacing Fear With Self-Trust and Emotional Stability
Becoming the Anchor, Not the Storm

When a man is ruled by unhealed emotions, he becomes unstable—
easily triggered, reactive in love, and unpredictable in leadership.

But when a man is grounded in emotional stability, everything changes:

- His presence becomes magnetic

- His words carry weight

- His relationships deepen

- His decisions are calm, not chaotic

- His confidence is unshakable

But to become that man, you must stop being ruled by fear—
And start building a relationship with the one person who will never leave you: yourself.

Fear Comes From Disconnection

When you feel unsafe within, you fear everything outside:

- You fear being abandoned

- You fear being exposed

- You fear failure, rejection, or emotional discomfort

- You fear being too much or not enough

So you try to protect yourself with control, silence, avoidance, or domination.

But all fear really comes from one place:

The belief that you won't be able to handle what comes next.

What Is Self-Trust?

Self-trust is knowing:

- "No matter what happens, I won't abandon myself."

- "I can feel discomfort and not collapse."

- "I can speak honestly and still be worthy of love."

- "I can face conflict and remain grounded."

- "I don't need to manipulate or run—I can hold the tension."

This kind of trust doesn't come from talent.
It comes from daily choices—especially when it's hard.

How to Build Emotional Stability and Self-Trust

1. Keep Small Promises to Yourself
Every time you do what you said you would—wake up early, finish the workout, express your truth—you build trust. You become reliable in your own eyes.

2. Respond, Don't React
When emotions rise, practice the pause.
Breathe. Name the feeling. Then choose your response with clarity.
This turns chaos into consciousness.

3. Reframe the Fear
Instead of: "What if I mess up?"
Say: "If I mess up, I'll still have my own back. I'll grow. I'll own it."
This rewires your nervous system for safety.

4.   Show Up When It's Hard
Every time you lean in instead of check out—during conflict, discomfort, or truth-telling—you prove that you are safe within yourself.

5.   Talk to Yourself With Strength
Not criticism. Not sarcasm. Strength.

"You've got this."
"Breathe. Stay with it."
"You're allowed to feel this and still move forward."

Why It Matters

A man with self-trust can lead, love, and live with calm power.
He doesn't chase control—he carries clarity.
He doesn't fear emotion—he holds space for it.
He doesn't shrink under pressure—he breathes, grounds, and builds.

He becomes the man that others turn to in chaos.
He becomes the man his woman can be soft with.
He becomes the father who teaches through presence, not punishment.
He becomes the leader who doesn't need perfection—only alignment.

When you trust yourself, fear loses its grip.

When you stabilize your emotions, the world around you becomes easier to navigate
And that's when you finally stop surviving—
And start leading.

Chapter 3

Activities & Reflections: Emotional Power

Learning to Connect, Not Control

1. Emotional Vocabulary Builder

Most men were taught only a few emotions: happy, angry, fine.

Your task:

Write down 10 emotions you've felt in the past 7 days.
Use a feelings chart or just describe the emotion as best you can.

For each emotion, reflect and answer:

- What triggered this?

- What did I do with the emotion?

2. Trigger Mapping Worksheet

Step 1: Identify 3 common emotional triggers
(e.g. being ignored, criticized, disrespected).

Step 2: For each trigger, journal your responses:

- Where do I feel it in my body?
- What past memory does it connect to?
- What belief does it activate in me?
- What is a more grounded response I can practice next time?

3. Conflict Communication Practice

Think of a recent moment you avoided a difficult conversation or exploded emotionally.

Now, rewrite that moment using emotionally intelligent language:

"I feel ___when ___because ___What I need is ___"

Practice reading it aloud until it feels natural.
(Optional: Record yourself and listen back.)

4. Calm Confidence Ritual

Create a daily 5-minute grounding routine to build emotional control:

- 1 minute deep breathing

- 2 minutes journaling your emotional state

- 1 minute speaking a self-affirmation such as: "I am safe. I lead myself."

- 1 minute silence or reflection

Do this for 5 days and journal how it affects your ability to stay centered.

Chapter 4
Real Leadership In Love

Building Honest, Purposeful Relationships
Love is not a reward.
It's not a status symbol.
And it's not something you "earn" through perfection,
performance, or possession.

Love is a mirror.
It reflects the deepest truths you've accepted—or ignored—
within yourself.

And for many men, that reflection has been hard to face.

Because no one taught you how to lead in love.
They taught you how to pursue.
How to impress.
How to control, suppress, or avoid.
But not how to show up with clarity, confidence, and emotional maturity.

This chapter is not about "getting the girl."
It's about becoming the kind of man who can lead, build, and sustain real love—with purpose and depth.

Why Leadership in Love Matters

When a man is unhealed, disconnected, or emotionally inconsistent, he:
- Chooses women based on chemistry, not character
- Reacts to conflict with ego or avoidance
- Repeats toxic cycles that mimic his past wounds
- Sabotages real connection with games, fear, or emotional shutdown

But when a man is grounded and growing?

- He sets the tone for connection
- He builds emotional safety
- He communicates clearly, not defensively
- He leads—not by control, but by example
- He knows when to pursue and when to walk away
- He chooses alignment over attachment

Love becomes less of a battlefield… and more of a partnership.

The Masculine Role in Modern Love

Let's be clear: leadership in love isn't about dominance.
It's not about taking power away.
It's about offering direction, safety, and clarity—so love
can grow with intention.

Your role is not to "fix" her.
Your role is to lead yourself so well that your relationship
becomes a reflection of your integrity.

You are the vision-holder, the pace-setter, the protector of
emotional standards.
Not because she can't lead—but because you won't avoid
your own responsibility anymore.

Real Love Requires Real Character

This chapter will show you how to:

- Let go of situationships and emotional chaos
- Identify and attract emotionally mature partners
- Understand the difference between attraction and alignment
- Lead your relationships with clarity, consistency, and truth
- See commitment not as a trap—but as a container for growth

Because the man who fears love ends up chasing pleasure.
But the man who understands love?
He builds something unbreakable.

What Leadership in Love Looks Like

A high-value man does not linger in emotional gray zones.
He gets clear. He gets honest. He chooses alignment over
attention.

He's not afraid to:

Ask, "What are we building together?"

Say no to a temporary connection if it blocks long-term
vision.

Walk away from what feels good but isn't growing him.

Take responsibility for the energy he allows in his life.

He doesn't ghost.
He doesn't breadcrumb.
He doesn't string people along for comfort or convenience.

He leads with clarity.

**How to Recognize and Pursue Emotionally Mature Women
Choosing Partners Who Build With You—Not Break You**

Once you begin healing and reclaiming your masculine
identity, your taste in women will naturally evolve.
You'll stop being drawn to chaos, neediness, or surface-
level attraction—and start craving depth, stability, and
partnership.

But recognizing an emotionally mature woman requires
that you first become an emotionally mature man.

You attract what you reflect.
And you tolerate what you believe you deserve.

Signs of an Emotionally Mature Woman

1. She Communicates With Clarity, Not Games
She doesn't rely on manipulation, silence, or drama to get her needs met.
She says what she means—and listens with respect.

2. She Has Emotional Self-Awareness
She owns her triggers and doesn't project blame.
She's done (or is doing) the work to understand her wounds and patterns.

3. She Respects Your Space and Direction
She doesn't try to control you, fix you, or make you her project.
She supports your mission and maintains her own.

4. She Holds Standards, Not Ultimatums
She knows what she wants and is clear about it,
but she doesn't force, beg, or chase.

5. She's Secure, Not Perfect
She's not afraid to be vulnerable, express affection, or let
you lead.
But she also takes full responsibility for her own growth.

Signs She May Not Be Emotionally Ready

- Constant emotional highs and lows

- Avoids real conversations

- Uses sex or silence as tools for control

- Criticizes instead of communicates

- Is easily offended and difficult to reassure

- Lacks boundaries—or disrespects yours

- Needs you to "make her happy" instead of creating her own inner peace

You can feel it in your nervous system: she either brings calm or chaos.
And the man you're becoming no longer has room for emotional instability masked as "chemistry."

Pursuing with Purpose

If you want a woman who meets you with maturity, you must also meet her with leadership.
That means:

- Initiating with clear intent
- Being upfront about your values and goals
- Asking meaningful questions—not just making moves
- Setting the emotional tone through honesty, boundaries, and consistency
- Not rushing intimacy—choosing connection over conquest

Not rushing intimacy—choosing connection over conquest

Emotionally mature women don't need a perfect man.
They need a present one. A grounded one. A clear one.

A man who doesn't confuse pressure with leadership.
A man who doesn't fear depth, distance, or directness.
A man who doesn't run when it's time to be real.

You Are Not Here to Be Chosen—You Are Here to Choose

Stop waiting for a woman to validate you.
Start choosing the kind of woman who aligns with your healing, your mission, and your future family.

You're not just building a relationship.

You're building a foundation—and it starts with who you allow to stand beside you.

The Difference Between Attraction and Alignment
Choosing What Grows You—Not Just What Excites You

There's a moment in every man's journey where he must make a critical shift:
From chasing chemistry… to choosing alignment.

Attraction is instinctive.
It's immediate, emotional, and often impulsive.

But alignment?
That's intentional.
That's built.
That's what creates legacy.

> Attraction gets your attention.
> Alignment builds your future.

When you chase attraction without alignment, you end up in the same patterns—beautiful, exciting, or passionate… but ultimately unsustainable.

What Is Attraction?
Attraction is:

- Chemistry

- Physical or emotional magnetism

- Familiar energy (even if it's unhealthy)

- Excitement driven by novelty or fantasy

- The adrenaline of the chase

But attraction alone cannot hold a relationship.
It can spark desire—but not direction.
It can ignite passion—but not peace.

Many men confuse attraction with connection.
And they wonder why things feel intense at first,
but unravel just as fast.

What Is Alignment?
Alignment is:

- Shared values

- Emotional maturity

- Compatible life visions

- Mutual respect and boundaries

- Safety, clarity, and growth

Alignment isn't always "sexy" at first—it doesn't come with the chaos, confusion, or highs and lows that many men were conditioned to associate with love.

But it lasts.
It builds.
It stabilizes.

Alignment means choosing someone who walks beside you, not just someone who turns you on.

Why Men Often Confuse the Two

Many men grew up around dysfunction. So when they feel
calm, safe, and respected—they mistake it for boredom.

They say:
"She's too nice."
"There's no spark."
"It just doesn't feel intense."

But often, what they're really saying is:

  "She doesn't trigger the wounds I'm used to reacting to."

That's not a red flag.
That's a sign of emotional healing.

It's time to stop confusing drama with desire.
Stop mistaking chaos for chemistry.
And stop choosing what feels exciting over what feels true.

How to Choose Alignment Over Attraction Alone

1.   Know What You Want
Have a clear vision of the relationship you want to build—
not just the woman you want to have.
Does she fit into your long-term life or just your short-term
pleasure?

2.   Ask the Right Questions
What are her values?
How does she handle stress, conflict, or rejection?
Does she inspire you to grow or tempt you to regress?

3.   Slow Down the Physical
Sexual energy can cloud discernment.
Build emotional and spiritual connection first.
Let clarity lead the pace.

4.   Don't Chase Familiar Pain

If she reminds you of someone who hurt you—or if the pattern feels too familiar—pause.
Is this attraction… or an unhealed trauma loop?

5.   Choose Peace Over Pressure

If you feel grounded, open, and seen in her presence—
you're on the right path.
If you feel anxious, unsure, or like you're performing… it's not alignment.

Choose With Your Future In Mind

You're not just choosing a partner.
You're choosing:

- The energy you wake up to every day

- The mother of your children (if that's in your path)

- The emotional environment you'll live in

- The person who will walk with you through storms

Don't just choose what excites you.
Choose what elevates you.

Leading in Love
Setting the Tone, Vision, and Direction in Relationships

Leadership isn't something you turn on in the workplace
and turn off in your relationship.

If you want a powerful, peaceful, purpose-driven
partnership—
you must lead it.

Not with control.
Not with ego.
Not with manipulation.

But with clarity, consistency, and intention.

A high-value man doesn't wait to be told what to do.
He sets the emotional tone.
He holds the relational standard.
He moves with purpose—and invites his partner into
alignment with it.

Because when a man is grounded, the relationship becomes safe.
And when a relationship is safe, it can grow into something extraordinary.

3 Core Pillars of Masculine Leadership in Relationships

1.   Vision
You lead with a long-term view.
You don't just go with the flow—you build a path.

"This is the kind of love I'm building. These are my values. This is where I'm going. Does that align with you?"

2.   Tone

You set the emotional climate.
Is the relationship tense or peaceful? Distant or intentional?

A man in his leadership doesn't allow emotional chaos to become the norm.
He leads with maturity.

3.   Direction

You make choices with clarity.
You don't linger in "what are we?" for months.
You move things forward—or you respectfully walk away.

You invite commitment—not through pressure, but through your presence.

Masculine Leadership Isn't Loud—It's Rooted

Real leadership isn't bossy.
It doesn't bark orders.
It doesn't seek to overpower.

It listens.
It adapts.
It makes hard decisions with calm energy.
It invites—not demands—trust.

And when a woman feels your consistent leadership, she
softens. She opens. She follows—
not out of obligation, but out of trust in your direction.

Practical Ways to Lead in Love

Plan intentional time together (don't just rely on convenience)

Bring up important conversations before they become problems

Set standards early (respect, honesty, communication, etc.)

Take initiative during conflict ("Let's pause and come back to this")

Communicate your needs and boundaries with maturity

Encourage her growth without trying to "fix" or lead her life

You lead the relationship not by controlling her— But by controlling yourself
and setting the energetic foundation of the bond.

Love Needs Leadership

Without leadership, love becomes reactive, chaotic, or stagnant.
With leadership, love becomes purposeful, expansive, and alive.

And remember:

Leadership is not something you're given.
It's something you earn—through your presence, your integrity, and your consistency.

Lead in love the way you lead your mission:
With heart.
With structure.
And with unwavering intention.

Why Commitment Is Not a Trap – It's a Tool for Evolution Becoming the Man Who Grows Through Devotion, Not Avoidance

There's a common fear among modern men:

"If I commit, I'll lose my freedom."
"If I commit, I'll get hurt."
"If I commit, I'll be stuck."

But that fear isn't about commitment.
It's about what commitment demands:
depth, vulnerability, consistency, and emotional responsibility.

Commitment doesn't trap a man.
It reveals him.

And for the man willing to lean into it,
commitment becomes the very force that forges his greatness.

What Commitment Actually Does for a Man

1. It Grounds You in Something Bigger Than Ego
When you're devoted to something beyond yourself—your woman, your family, your future—
you stop making impulsive decisions.
You start living intentionally.

2. It Reveals Your Emotional Maturity
It's easy to show up when it's fun.
Commitment tests how you show up when it's not.
That's when character is built.

3. It Forces You to Grow
Real love reflects your shadows.
It shows you your wounds, your blind spots, your tendencies to run.
It demands that you evolve—or repeat the cycle.

4. It Makes You a Legacy-Builder
Any man can chase. Few can create something that lasts.
Commitment turns desire into devotion.
It turns love into leadership.

Signs You're Ready for Real Commitment

- You don't run at the first sign of conflict
- You're willing to grow with someone, not just impress them
- You've stopped romanticizing emotional chaos
- You're clear about what you want and what you stand for
- You understand that relationships require repair, not just chemistry
- You no longer confuse peace with boredom

Commitment as a Container for Masculine Expansion

A strong man doesn't fear commitment—he uses it as a mirror.
He lets it show him where he still needs healing.
He lets it shape him into the kind of man who can love deeply without losing himself.
He lets it stretch his capacity for patience, presence, and leadership.

Because in commitment, there's no place to hide.

And that's the point
That's where the rebuild becomes real.

Your Power Is in Your Devotion

Devotion isn't desperation.
It's direction.

It says: "I'm choosing this path on purpose. And I will show up every day—
not because I have to, but because I choose to."

That's not weakness.
That's masculinity fully matured.

Chapter 4
Activities & Reflections: Real Leadership in Love

1. Relationship Inventory

Reflect on your past 1–3 relationships or dating experiences. For each, journal:

What patterns repeated?
What emotional wounds showed up?
Did I lead with purpose—or react from pain?
What would I do differently now as a grounded, emotionally intelligent man?

Objective: Identify the cycles you're here to break.

2. The Alignment List

Write down 10 traits you desire in a long-term partner (character, values, energy).
Then list 10 traits YOU must embody to attract and sustain that kind of connection.

Reflection Question:
Are you currently aligned with the love you say you want?

3. Communication Rehearsal

Choose one difficult truth or emotion you've avoided expressing in a relationship—past or present.
Write out how you would express it now, using emotional maturity:

"I feel ___when ___because ___What I need is ___."

4. Devotion vs. Desperation

Journal on the difference:

- What does devotion look like in a masculine relationship?

- What does desperation or chasing look like?

- Where have I confused the two in my own love life?

- How will I lead love differently moving forward?

Chapter 5
Building a Man's Legacy
Discipline, Purpose & Presence

There comes a point in every man's life where the desire
for validation fades…
and the hunger for legacy begins.

You no longer want to just be liked.
You want to be respected.
You want to matter—to stand for something real.
You want to know that your life means something beyond
what you consume, post, or achieve.

But legacy isn't about how many people know your name.
It's about what your presence builds and protects.

A man's legacy is not found in his words—
it's found in his discipline, his purpose, and his presence.

What Is Legacy, Really?

Legacy is the emotional, spiritual, and practical impact you leave behind:

- The way your children feel when they hear your name
- The standards you set for love, manhood, and leadership The character you carry when no one is watching
- The emotional safety you create for your partner and family
- The mission you commit to with consistency and integrity

Legacy is not about what you collect. It's about what you contribute.

Why Most Men Struggle With Purpose
You can't build a legacy when:

- You're constantly distracted

- You have no clear mission

- You chase pleasure more than principles

- You live in cycles of starting and stopping

- You keep numbing the part of you that knows you're

  meant for more

A man without purpose becomes his own worst enemy.
He becomes reactive, impulsive, emotionally unstable, and
secretly ashamed.

But when a man finds his why—his reason to rise, lead,
and give—everything changes.

He stops wasting time.
He stops seeking validation.
He starts building with focus and fire.

Creating a Vision for Your Life Beyond Dating

Building a Future That Doesn't Revolve Around Women, Ego, or Escape

You weren't born to chase women.
You weren't created to endlessly scroll, react, impress, or survive.
You were made to build. To lead. To create impact.

But many men stay stuck in a cycle where their lives revolve around:

- Proving themselves to women

- Escaping through entertainment, porn, or substances

- Reacting to life instead of designing it

- Living in short-term emotion instead of long-term purpose

Why Vision Matters

Without vision:

- You chase what feels good instead of what builds you
- You settle for who you are instead of becoming who you're meant to be
- You keep wasting time on things and people that don't align
- You live distracted, directionless, and drained

But when you have vision:

- You start making powerful decisions
- You attract alignment instead of chaos

- You create structure and clarity
- You feel alive—not just entertained
- You become magnetic to the right opportunities and people

A man with vision becomes dangerous—in the best way. Because he no longer needs attention… he commands respect.

What Does Your Vision Look Like?

Ask yourself:

What kind of man do I want to be in 10 years?

What values will shape my life?

What kind of relationships do I want to lead?

What kind of example do I want to be for the next generation?

What impact do I want to make in my family, community, or business?

What kind of physical, emotional, and spiritual legacy do I want to leave behind?

This is not about perfection—it's about alignment. When you know where you're going, you stop settling for what holds you back.

Your Vision Is Your Filter

Once your vision is clear, everything in your life can be evaluated by one question:

"Does this serve the man I'm becoming?"

That habit you're holding on to
That situationship you keep entertaining
That job, environment, or friend group
That behavior you know is draining your energy and
confidence

Keep only what serves the vision.
Everything else? It goes.

Because legacy requires sacrifice.
And discipline begins the moment you realize your future
matters more than your comfort.

Daily Discipline

Mastering Your Body, Mind, Money & Mission

You don't rise to your goals—you fall to your level of discipline.
And in a world that promotes distraction, emotional comfort, and chasing validation, discipline isn't just a habit.

Discipline is a masculine superpower.

Without it, your goals stay as ideas.
Your confidence stays fragile.
Your relationships stay unstable.
And your life never reaches the level you feel in your spirit you were meant for.

This section is about reclaiming your masculine edge—through the daily disciplines that build a man's body, mind, money, and mission.

Discipline Is Self-Respect

Every time you:

- Hit snooze when you said you'd get up
- Skip the workout you committed to
- Numb out instead of doing the work
- Betray your own word to yourself

You weaken trust with the man in the mirror.

But every time you follow through—especially when it's hard—you rise.
Your self-respect grows.
And you become the kind of man who no longer needs external approval—because he has internal authority.

Discipline Over the Body

Your body is your temple—and your training ground for self-mastery.

- Work out consistently (not for aesthetics, but for strength, discipline, and presence)
- Eat with intention, not emotion
- Get proper sleep—protect your energy
- Eliminate substances and habits that weaken your clarity

When you master your body, you sharpen your focus, your sex drive, your emotional control, and your masculine fire.

Discipline Over the Mind

Your mind is your command center. Keep it strong.

- Start the day without social media
- Feed your mind with content that stretches and sharpens you
- Meditate or journal—create internal space
- Challenge your limiting beliefs daily
- Take time in silence to think, reflect, and direct your energy

If your mind is weak, you'll react.
If your mind is trained, you'll lead.

Discipline Over Money

A man with no control over his money will always feel powerless.

- Track your income and spending
- Save and invest with strategy
- Delay gratification to build long-term peace
- Stop trying to impress—start building wealth
- Respect money by learning how it works and how to multiply it

Discipline over money leads to options, freedom, and impact.

Discipline Over Mission

Your purpose needs structure—not just passion.

- Set clear goals and break them into daily action
- Create routines that support focus and momentum
- Eliminate distractions that steal your energy and clarity
- Build consistency, even when motivation fades
- Show up when it's hard—not just when it's convenient

Your mission doesn't care how you feel—it rewards how you show up.

The Daily Standard of a High-Value Man

Discipline is not about being robotic. It's about being aligned.

- Wake up with purpose.
- Train with intention.
- Speak with clarity.
- Work with focus.
- Rest with peace.
- Repeat with consistency.

You don't need more motivation.
You need a standard you refuse to drop below.

And when you live by that standard—you become unstoppable.

Replacing Escapism with Responsibility
Why Real Men Don't Run—They Rise

Every man hits a point in life where he faces the mirror and asks:

"Am I building... or escaping?"

It's easy to look disciplined on the outside—hitting goals, making money, getting attention.
But if behind the scenes you're drowning in porn, alcohol, drugs, cheating, lies, or emotional shutdown—

You're not in control.
You're not free.
You're running.
You're numbing.
You're slowly destroying the man you're working so hard to become.

This is not a guilt trip.

It's a wake-up call.
Because you can't build legacy while running from responsibility.

What Is Escapism?

Escapism is anything you use to avoid feeling, facing, or fixing what's real.

It might look like:
- A drink every night that turns into many
- Casual sex or cheating to avoid emotional intimacy
- Porn to avoid the discipline of connection
- Drugs to silence your restlessness or pain
- Video games or social media to numb your ambition
- Overworking to avoid your emotional life
- Emotional detachment so you don't have to be accountable in relationships

Escapism feels good in the moment.

But over time, it erodes your:
- Focus
- Integrity
- Emotional strength
- Relationship trust
- Health
- Leadership
- Legacy

Why Men Escape

Men escape because they were never taught how to:
- Sit with discomfort
- Regulate emotion
- Face consequences without collapse
- Heal shame without addiction
- Ask for help without feeling weak

So we create patterns.
We build secret lives.
We self- sabotage.

We call it "just letting off steam" or "boys being boys"—
but deep down, we know:

We're hiding.

From Numbing to Leading

A man in his power no longer escapes pain.
He uses it to elevate.
He asks:

- "What is this discomfort trying to show me?"
- "What responsibility have I been avoiding?"
- "Where am I playing small by numbing instead of facing?"
- "What am I afraid to feel—and what would happen if I actually sat with it?"

How to Replace Escapism with Masculine Responsibility

1.   Identify Your Escape Route

What's your go-to? Alcohol? Sex? Scrolling? Anger? Call it out. Don't justify it. Own it.

2.   Interrupt the Cycle

Replace the habit with presence.

When the urge hits— pause.

Breathe. Journal. Move your body. Call someone.

Break the loop with awareness, not shame.

3.   Create a Standard, Not a Story

Stop saying "I'm trying to cut back."

Start saying "This is no longer who I am."

Raise the standard for your energy, focus, and integrity.

4.   Sit in the Discomfort

Learn to feel fully without needing to numb.

Use breathwork, meditation, cold exposure, or journaling to stay present with the emotion until it moves through.

5.   Replace Numbing With Responsibility

Instead of drinking—face the conflict.

Instead of cheating—communicate or walk away.

Instead of escaping—take action on your mission.

Responsibility is not a burden. It's your masculine birthright.

You Can't Numb and Lead at the Same Time

A man cannot lead his family, his purpose, or his future if he's secretly at war with himself.

You don't need to be perfect.
You need to be present.
You need to be honest.
You need to be responsible.

Because your habits shape your identity.
And your identity builds your legacy.

It's time to stop running.
It's time to rise.

Becoming the Man Your Future Family, Partner & Community Can Depend On

The New Standard of Masculinity

Every man has a choice:
To live for the weekend...
or to live for a legacy.
To seek escape...
or to become the anchor.
To remain reactive, avoidant, and emotionally scattered...
or to step into the kind of strength the world can lean on.

This final section is about rising into masculine
dependability—
not perfection, but presence.

Because one day, someone will look to you and ask:

"Can I count on you when things get hard?"
"Will you protect, not just provide?"
"Will you lead with love and not with fear?"

And the man who can answer yes—he is the new standard.

What It Means to Be Dependable as a Man

It means:
- Your word holds weight
- Your emotions are stable—not suppressed, but led
- You don't fold under pressure—you refocus
- You show up when you say you will
- You take responsibility without excuses
- You protect peace in your home and relationships
- You're emotionally safe and spiritually grounded

This is what every good woman wants in a partner. It's what children need in a father.
It's what communities need in a leader.
And it's what your own soul has been craving from you all along.

Building the Legacy of a High-Value Man

You don't have to be rich.
You don't have to be famous.
You don't have to be perfect.

But you must be consistent.

You must be the man who:
- Doesn't hide behind lust, lies, or ego

- Doesn't silence his heart to appear strong

- Doesn't blame, avoid, or shrink in the face of hard conversations

- Doesn't destroy what he loves just to feed what he's avoiding

Instead, you must be the man who:

- Speaks truth and follows through
- Stands for what's right even when it's hard
- Creates emotional safety at home
- Protects what he builds
- Leads with a heart that's healed and hands that are ready

That is legacy.
That is manhood.
That is the rebuild.

Walk in Strength – The New Masculine Standard

You're not here to be perfect.
You're here to be solid.
To be grounded.
To be dependable.
To be a man of presence, protection, and purpose.

Because the world doesn't just need more men. It needs
more good men.
More healed men.
More high-value men.
Men who lead not by force, but by example.

And that man?
He's not waiting to be told what to do.
He's already rising.

- **Chapter 5 Activities & Reflections: Building a Man's Legacy**

1. Vision Crafting Exercise

Write out your 10-Year Legacy Vision by answering:

Who am I as a man in 10 years?

What do people feel when they hear my name?

What values do I stand for?

What am I building or protecting with my life?

Be as detailed and bold as possible. This becomes your internal compass.

2. Legacy Filters

List out:

3 habits

3 relationships

3 daily routines

...that either support or sabotage your legacy.

For each one, label it:

- **Keep** – Supports who I'm becoming

- **Restructure** – Needs improvement

- **Eliminate** – Holds me back

Reflect:
"Am I living aligned with the man I want to be remembered as?"

2. Daily Discipline Tracker

For the next 7 days, track these foundational masculine disciplines:

- Wake-up time (no snooze)

- Physical training or movement

- No digital distraction during set blocks (work, morning, night)

- One action aligned with your purpose (small or big)

- End-of-day journal reflection (1–2 sentences only)

At the end of 7 days, rate yourself 1–10 on consistency and reflect on what improved in your mindset, mood, or focus.

4. Your Leadership Code

Write your personal Leadership Code—a list of 5 non-negotiables that define how you lead yourself and others.

Examples:

- I lead by example, not by control.

- I finish what I start.

- I choose alignment over approval.

- I protect my peace and energy.

- I serve with strength and humility.

Print it. Post it. Live it.

Chapter 6:
Brotherhood & Belonging
Reclaiming Masculine Connection in a World of Isolation

You weren't meant to do this alone.
No matter how strong, disciplined, or purpose-driven you become—

There will be days when you feel
Tired.
Disconnected.
Misunderstood.
Tempted to go back to the old life.
To quit. To isolate. To numb.

And the greatest lie men have been told is this:

"You have to figure it out by yourself."

You don't.
And in fact, if you try—you'll eventually break.
Because masculine strength isn't just built through solitude.
It's forged in brotherhood.

This chapter is your invitation to stop isolating, stop
pretending, and start building or joining a circle of men
who push you forward, call you higher, and walk beside
you in purpose.

The Crisis of the Lone Wolf

Most men grow up learning to suppress emotion and compete for power.
So we become "lone wolves"—strong but disconnected.
Capable but deeply lonely.

We:

- Don't trust other men

- Assume we'll be judged if we open up

- Compare, compete, or avoid

- Carry burdens in silence

- Feel isolated in leadership, relationships, or healing

But the lone wolf eventually breaks down—either quietly through addiction and numbness, or loudly through burnout, rage, or collapse.

You were not built to walk alone.

Why Brotherhood Matters

When you're surrounded by strong, emotionally intelligent men:

- You don't have to carry your burden by yourself
- You get honest feedback when your ego tries to lead
- You're encouraged when you feel discouraged
- You're challenged to rise when you want to settle
- You're reminded of your mission when you lose focus
- You stop seeking validation—because you're surrounded by truth

Brotherhood is the mirror, the fire, and the covering.
It makes you sharper.
It keeps you accountable.
It keeps you aligned.

The Rebuild: What You've Become

You've made it through the storm—through the layers of pain, confusion, and silence that once defined your world.

But this isn't just the end of a book.
It's the beginning of the man you were always meant to become.

You've rebuilt...

- From passivity into purpose

- From ego into emotional strength

- From confusion into clarity

- From wounded reactions into grounded responses

- From fear of commitment into the courage to lead love

You've come face to face with your inner boy—and you chose not to run, numb, or avoid.
You chose to reparent him, heal him, and rise above him.

You reclaimed your masculinity—not the version the world distorted, but the one rooted in honor, structure, and direction.

You now understand that emotional power is not weakness.
It's mastery.
It's the ability to hold steady in chaos.
To feel deeply without losing yourself.
To lead without needing to control.

You've learned to stand in love—not just fall into it.
You've chosen leadership in relationships, in family, and in legacy.
You no longer chase women to feel validated or run from intimacy when it gets too real.

You build.
You lead.
You protect.

And what's more—you've become the man others can
trust, follow, and feel safe with.
Your future family will feel it.
Your partner will feel it.
Your community will feel it.

Keep Rebuilding

This isn't the end.
The rebuild doesn't stop. It deepens.

Every day, you are faced with a choice:
To show up with integrity
To lead with calm confidence
To walk in the values you've chosen
To keep expanding, evolving, and leading with love

The New You Is Not a Dream.

He's here.
He's awake.
He's you.

You are not who you used to be.
You are not a product of your wounds.
You are a man who faced himself and rose anyway.

That is what makes you powerful.

www.ingramcontent.com/pod-product-compliance
Lightning Source LLC
Chambersburg PA
CBHW070916130626
46555CB00001B/154